Turquoise and Six-Guns

The Story of Cerrillos, New Mexico

by Marc Simmons

The Sunstone Press
Santa Fe, New Mexico

NEW AND REVISED EDITION
Second Printing 1975

*Front Cover illustration intended only as an artistic inter-
pretation of the Cerrillos railroad and station during the
boom era, and should not be relied upon as a true repre-
sentation of same.*

Book Design by Rachel Abrams
Index by Wm. Farrington

ISBN 0-913270-33-4
Library of Congress Catalog Card Number: 74-84842

Printed In The United States Of America

To The Memory of
Kathryn Q. García
(Cochití Pueblo)

TABLE OF CONTENTS

PREFACE

Los Cerrillos, the town of the Little Hills, straddles the deeply cut and poorly watered Rio Galisteo near its junction with the San Marcos Arroyo. Away to the south looms the round-shouldered bulk of the Ortiz Range, and beyond, the purple hump of Sandia Mountain. At the end of Main Street, past the ghostly ruins of the old Palace Hotel, the view stretches unimpeded league upon league down the narrow trough of the Galisteo Basin until, finally, it is arrested by the violet rim of the Sierra de Jémez. To the north, the cluster of knobby hills from which the town draws its name forms an irregular wall broken now and again by yawning canyon mouths. And westward, the eye follows the course of the Galisteo as it skirts the edge of the Cerrillos Badlands, beyond which the river disappears in a northerly direction toward its headwaters on Glorieta Baldy.

The rock-ribbed hills surrounding Cerrillos are honeycombed with mineshafts and it is these mines that have shaped the history of the town and of the district over which it presides. The Pueblo Indians for untold ages took out turquoise; the Spaniards in their turn found gold, silver and lead; and finally, the Anglo-Americans exploited all of these in addition to copper, zinc and coal. Mining gave life to Cerrillos and to neighboring towns such as Bonanza City, Carbonateville, Waldo and Madrid. And when the boom passed and the mines closed, that life ebbed away. Scattered over the hills and in the valleys everywhere are skeletal remains of mining activity: deserted buildings, black and foreboding entrances to shafts, broken tools and equipment, fallen timbers from the windlasses, gallows and hoist houses, tailing dumps and slag heaps. These offer silent testimony to the once prosperous past of the Cerrillos mining district.

The first edition of *Turquoise & Six-Guns* appeared in 1968, privately printed by the author. It enjoyed a modest success and within a short time went out of print. At the suggestion of the Sunstone Press, the writer undertook to revise and expand the earlier work, giving greater emphasis to the Cerrillos mining district as a whole and calling attention to some of the lesser known ghost camps that enjoyed a brief but tempestuous life during the boom period. Moreover, a significant number of photographs, some historical, others recent, have been added to the present account, as have several line drawings kindly prepared by Frank Turley.

I

Thanks are owed to photographer Bart Durham, who not only assisted in assembling the illustrations but who also generously gave the author access to his collection of printed materials on the history of Cerrillos. Stephany Eger, History Librarian of the Museum of New Mexico, and the staff of the New Mexico State Records Center and Archives helped in locating sources in their collections. Photographer Buddy Mays contributed photos of the ghost town of Madrid, and Natalie Beckman prepared the map. Finally, I should acknowledge that parts of this work were composed at the Crossed Sabers Ranch of General and Mrs. Sam Goodwin on the banks of the Rio Galisteo and at the Tedlock Hacienda further north in the Cerrillos Badlands.

Marc Simmons
January 1, 1974

"We have all the saloons here we need, but a good stock of groceries and general merchandise is an absolute necessity."

From an editorial in
THE CERRILLOS RUSTLER, 1894

I

In the small range of camel-humped hills north of Cerrillos is one of the heaviest concentrations of minerals to be found in the Southwest. Here igneous rocks, products of volcanic activity, have intruded through layers of sediment or in their motion have tilted vast sheets of sandstone and mudstone on end. East of the hills, along Highway 14, erosion has exposed walls and pillars of red, pink and orange rock, creating a natural park that geologists have termed a miniature "Garden of the Gods." In some places water slicing through the topsoil has brought to light dikes and plugs of black lava and has seamed the earth with hollow canyons or steep-walled arroyos.

Scattered through the geologic formations of the Cerrillos district are two kinds of fossils: bones of ancient mammals and petrified wood. Scientists who enjoy stitching skeletons together have identified one strange animal of the late Eocene period as a titanotheres, a creature they describe as a "moronic rhinoceros."

The petrified wood, mostly huge pine, is dispersed over several square miles east of Cerrillos. It is so abundant that old maps refer to the area as the petrified forest. In the days of the mining boom, many families drove buggies out from town to picnic and to view the geological curiosity of wood turned to stone. A Mr. Cavalier led one such party in the summer of 1894, and the local newspaper reported upon a disquieting mishap. *"In coming home from the petrified forest, the vehicle tipped over on a bad piece of road – there was some little excitement but no damage was done. The ladies say, however, that Mr. Cavalier must furnish valid certificates and references as an engineer competent to safely handle a mule team before they will again entrust their precious selves to his charge."*

To many people familiar with a greener, softer country, the Galisteo Basin and the uplands on its margin are a bleak and arid waste, scarcely relieved by the thin covering of forage grasses and stunted clumps of cedar and piñon. The sprinkling of cholla and prickly pear cactus lends weight to the opinion that this land is little more than a desert. Yet here and there one unexpectedly meets springs and natural pools, and even occasionally a running stream. To be sure, much of the water is alkaline, but still it can be used for drinking. The Indians once turned some of it into irrigation ditches.

Pueblo Indian, Spaniard and Anglo miner accepted what the environment of Cerrillos had to offer, complained scarcely at all of nature's apparent deficiencies, and accepted the modest prosperity which the country and their own efforts bestowed upon them.

II

The Tano Indians were the first people in the Cerrillos area about whom we have definite knowledge. Their pueblos, large and small, were sprinkled randomly throughout the middle Galisteo Basin at least by the mid-fourteenth century. Scores of ruins might lead us to believe that the Tano population was once numerous, but archaeologists guess these sites were occupied at different times and that at no one period did the Indians number more than a few thousand. Some of the old pueblos may have been abandoned when the farm lands wore out; a few, such as Burnt Corn Ruin five miles east of Cerrillos, show evidence of having been destroyed in battle. In any case, the people did a good deal of shifting about, leaving piles of tumbled stones, broken potsherds and discarded tools of rock and bone as a record of their passing.

The most eloquent testimony to the Tanos' artistic talent and to the richness of their ceremonial life can be found in their petroglyphs or rock carvings. Hundreds, perhaps thousands, decorate volcanic dikes and protected sandstone faces. This primitive art is characterized by a wide diversity of forms: figures of humans and gods, religious masks and other sacred paraphernalia, animals, birds, reptiles, flora, celestial bodies, and symbols of all kinds. Prominent on many of these stone picture books is the feathered snake, a deity popular among the ancient Aztecs of Mexico as well as among the Pueblos. At the summit of one conspicuous hill on the northern edge of the basin, black basalt boulders provided convenient tablets for inscribing successes relating to human fertility rites.

In prehistoric times small pueblos probably existed within sight of Cerrillos. Game was fairly plentiful, and Indian farmers planted crops on the level ground bordering both sides of the Galisteo River above town. Since the stream channel was not so deeply eroded as it is today, we can surmise that water was funneled off in small ditches to irrigate the fields of corn, beans, squash, pumpkins and tobacco. In addition, the piñon forests in the foothills of the Ortiz periodically gave forth their yields of fat nuts, a basic staple of the Indian diet.

When the Spaniards first saw them, the Tanos dwelled in four of five major pueblos, including San Marcos, Galisteo, San Cristobal, and San Lázaro. The nearest to the site of Cerrillos was San Marcos, located on the arroyo of the same name four miles to the northeast. It was known to the Indians as *Kunyaonweji*, meaning "Turquoise Pueblo," because of its proximity to the turquoise mines in the Cerrillos Hills. Other Indians seem to have recognized that the San Marcos people held first claim to the valuable deposits of blue stone and it is possible that anyone wishing to mine first sought permission from them.

San Marcos Pueblo, founded about A.D. 1350, was inhabited continuously until the great revolt of 1680. Several springs provided a constant water supply for domestic use, but the flow of the adjacent San Marcos Arroyo was scant and crops must have depended upon the irregular rainfall. Some farms were as much as two to three miles from the main village. Summer camps, where families lived near their fields, are marked today by broken pottery and corn grinding stones. Small heaps of rock scattered over a wide area are early Indian shrines. In these sacred places they may have placed blessed corn meal and other offerings to insure the needed rains for their agriculture.

III

Alvar Nuñez Cabeza de Vaca, shipwrecked on the coast of Texas with several companions, may have been the first Spaniard to approach the present boundaries of New Mexico. Somewhere in the vicinity of El Paso he found Indians in possession of beautiful turquoise stones that reportedly came from rich kingdoms to the north. Not long afterward, in 1539, Fray Marcos de Niza also saw turquoise specimens in northern Mexico and at the same time collected stories of golden cities which the natives said lay hidden beyond the limits of Spanish exploration.

The adventurer Francisco Vásquez de Coronado assembled a glittering company of noblemen and in 1540 set out with much fanfare to find the fabled cities of the north. Unfortunately, New Mexico proved a disappointment to Coronado since the treasured kingdoms were only legend. The Spaniards spent the winter at a pueblo north of present Albuquerque and in the spring ventured eastward to renew their search for wealth on the plains of Kansas. In all likelihood, the expedition passed over or near the site of Cerrillos. In fact, the Galisteo Basin in later times became the principal route for Spaniards traveling from the Rio Grande settlements to the buffalo plains.

Almost forty years after Coronado and his men passed by, a more humble party of Spaniards entered the Cerrillos district. The leaders were several Franciscan padres who had come to explore possibilities for opening missionary work. While at San Marcos Pueblo, one of the priests, Juan de Santa María, decided to return alone to Mexico City to make a report to his religious superiors. The Tano Indians, perhaps fearing that Father Santa María was going to seek soldiers who would come to conquer them, followed him southward and somewhere near the Sandia Mountains killed him while he rested under a piñon tree. The other padres, when they learned the fate of their brother, referred to San Marcos as the Pueblo of Malpartida, meaning the Village of Evil Parting, since it was from there that Father Santa María had started on his last journey.

Another explorer, Antonio de Espejo, visited the area in 1583 prospecting for mines, and it is known that he paused at San Marcos and other Tano towns. Of New Mexico he wrote exuberantly to the King, *"The earth is filled with gold, silver, and turquoise."*

Eight years later, Gaspar Castaño de Sosa halted at San Marcos and from there made a brief side excursion to the Cerrillos Hills where he examined some promising mineral deposits and collected rock specimens, probably from the turquoise pit on Mount Chalchihuitl. He also may have discovered a lead mine that was later worked by the Spaniards.

Spanish colonists established permanent settlements in New Mexico in 1598 but years elapsed before venturesome souls took up homes in the isolated Galisteo Basin. Very early, however, Franciscan padres erected missions among the pueblos of the Tano, and by the 1630s there were churches at the major villages. Sometime in the middle seventeenth century, Spanish farmers and ranchers began to move into the area and the district took the name Cerrillos, although there was no real community at this early date. It is likely that these colonists did not have a church or chapel of their own but attended religious services held by the Franciscans in nearby Indian pueblos.

Angered by oppressive Spanish rule, the Pueblo Indians of New Mexico rose in revolt in 1680. Some 400 colonists and 21 missionary friars met their deaths in one of the bloodiest uprisings ever to occur within the Spanish empire. At the first sign of trouble, the settlers around Cerrillos collected in a fortified hacienda belonging to Sargento Mayor Bernabé Marquez, which was situated on the San Marcos Arroyo not far from the Indian pueblo. With the hacienda under attack, an urgent message was sent to Santa Fe begging for aid. In response, on the night of August 12, a military force hastened down from the capital and rescued the beleaguered people, including Marquez, his wife, six children, a brother-in-law and seven servants. These few people from Cerrillos and a handful from the Española Valley were all that managed to escape to Santa Fe from the northern part of the province.

The capital itself soon came under siege as warriors from many pueblos joined in common cause against the Spaniards. In the forefront of the attack were the Tano, especially those from San Marcos and Galisteo Pueblos, who led the assault on the eastern suburb of Santa Fe and were responsible for the burning of San Miguel Church.

After five days of heavy fighting, the Spanish governor realized the hopelessness of his position and ordered the more than one thousand surviving colonists to begin a retreat southward. Not far from San Marcos, perhaps in the ruins of the Marquez hacienda, a council of war *(junta de guerra)* was called to organize the flight. A captured Indian confirmed that the Franciscan padres of the district had all been slain at Galisteo Pueblo, among them Father Manuel Tinoco, who had fled there from his station at San Marcos.

Ultimately all Spaniards who had not perished in the terrible revolt left New Mexico. The reconquest of the province did not take place until 1692, when a new governor and captain-general, Diego de Vargas, returned and reasserted control by the Spanish King. At this time it was found that many of the Tano Indians from the Cerrillos area had left their pueblos and moved into the old Governor's Palace and other buildings in Santa Fe abandoned in 1680. De Vargas was obliged to evict them and many of the Tano were placed in new villages north of Santa Fe. Only Galisteo Pueblo was refounded on its old site east of Cerrillos.

Probably few if any of the original Spanish colonists around Cerrillos returned to reclaim their old homes and property after the reconquest. Bernabé Marquez, for example, is known to have gone to Mexico City to live. One of the reconquering soldiers, Alonso Rael de Aguilar, received a land grant near Cerrillos from General De Vargas. Long afterward, the husband of Rael's granddaughter, Jose Miguel de la Peña, petitioned the governor in Santa Fe for possession of these lands. The request, made in 1788, read in part as follows:

> . . .*said piece of land at Los Cerrillos having been abandoned for*
> *so many years and said Don Alonso having lost the right he had*
> *to it, now sir I ask Your Excellency for the same in the name of*
> *his Majesty with all its entrances and exits, pastures and watering*
> *places, uses and customs, for me, my children, and heirs.* . . .

The petition was successful and on April 20, 1788, Governor Fernando de la Concha came in person from the capital and placed Peña in possession of his new grant. When land was assigned in this manner a standard ceremony was observed. The presiding official pointed out the boundaries of the grant while the person receiving the concession pulled up grass, threw rocks, and everyone, including the witnesses, joined in shouting, "*Viva el Rey!* Long Live the King!"

In December of 1804, another citizen, Cleito Miera, was awarded a land grant in the Cerrillos country, apparently just to the west of the property held by Miguel de la Peña. Others who received grants in later years were Pedro Bautista Pino, Salvador Martín, Manuel Delgado and Antonio Anaya. Pino was one of the most prominent political figures of his time, gaining renown as the only representative from New Mexico ever to serve in the Spanish parliament. For many years he maintained a hacienda around the springs and small stream of El Alamo on or near the present site of the Jarrott Ranch headquarters. The original Cerrillos land grant was close by on the east and, in fact, most of the Spanish population during colonial times resided on the north side of the hills rather than on the south, where the mining town of Cerrillos was founded in territorial days.

In any mining region stories of lost or buried treasure abound. Mention of Spanish gold mines near Cerrillos occurs frequently in the general histories and leads weekend fortune hunters to scour the hills for hidden wealth. Unfortunately, direct evidence that the Spaniards extracted any great amount of gold during colonial times is slim, although legend persists that some $3 million worth was mined and sent to Mexico. Undoubtedly some early exploitation of minerals was undertaken, but no real boom occurred in the Cerrillos parish until the nineteenth century, after New Mexico had become part of the Republic of Mexico. In 1823 a herder was tending his animals on the slopes of the Ortiz Mountains just south of Cerrillos when he picked up a stone to throw at one of his mules. The peculiar weight in his hand caused him to examine the rock with care and he discovered it was flecked with particles of gold. When word spread of the new bonanza, fortune hunters collected in the area and established the mining camp of Dolores, later called Old Placers.

The noted Santa Fe trader Josiah Gregg wrote in the 1840s that *"the only successful mines known in New Mexico at the present day, are those of gold, the most important one of which is that originally incorporated as El Real de Dolores,* but generally known by the significant name of El Placer. The quantity of gold extracted between the years 1832 and '35 could not have amounted to less than from $60,000 to $80,000 per annum. It is believed that the entire aggregate yield since the first discovery has exceeded half a million dollars."* The placers of the area (gold-carrying gravels) were laden with dust, grains and hefty nuggets of virgin metal. Some persons theorized that the gold originally accumulated in lodes or pockets, and that later it was spread over the surface of the country by volcanic activity or water erosion. For years prospectors searched the slopes and canyons of the Ortiz Mountains hoping to find an undisturbed hoard of yellow treasure, the mother lode.

*In Spanish times, the term *real*, literally "royal," was used to designate a mining camp because all minerals belonged to the King. He allowed his subjects to work the mines and received the "royal fifth" of all that was produced.

Gregg toured some of the Dolores mines and described what he saw:
During the process of these excavations, when such a depth has been reached as to render a ladder indispensable, a pole ten to fifteen feet long is cut full of notches for that purpose, and set diagonally in the orifice. In proportion as the pit becomes deeper, others are added, forming a somewhat precarious zigzag staircase, by which the agile miner descends and ascends without even using his hands to assist himself, although with a large load of earth upon his shoulders. [Figure 1] *It is in this way that most of the rubbish is extracted from these mines, as windlasses or machinery of any kind are rarely used.*

The winter season is generally preferred by the miners, for the facilities it affords of supplying the gold-washers with water in the immediate neighborhood of the operations; for the great scarcity of water about the mining regions is a very serious obstacle at other seasons to successful enterprise. Water in winter is obtained by melting a quantity of snow thrown into a sink with heated stones. Those employed as washers are very frequently the wives and children of the miners.

In 1846, the year New Mexico came under United States control, Lt. James W. Abert visited the mines south of Cerrillos and recorded what he saw. At the Dolores camp he found about 200 people engaged in mining or in tending great numbers of sheep and goats. In the Galisteo Basin and neighboring valleys he estimated 5,000 sheep were grazing. Dolores was described as a miserable collection of hovels whose citizens lived in abject poverty. Gold was abundant — everywhere the ground was pockmarked with holes and open shafts — but so much effort was needed to extract it and the tools were so primitive that few of the diggers could do more than manage to feed themselves on their profits. Abert saw *"many miserable looking wretches, clothed in rags, with an old piece of iron to dig the earth, and some gourds or horns of the mountain goats, to wash the sand. They sit all day at work, and at evenings repair to some tienda or store, where they exchange their gold for bread and meat."* Certainly this is not the picture of a prosperous gold camp.

Near Dolores Lt. Abert came upon a Frenchman who had staked a claim and constructed a crude mill for grinding ore.
This mill, a specimen of all others in the country, was of rather primitive construction. Large slabs of stone were used to floor a circular pit about 6 inches deep. In the center of this an axis was erected from which three beams projected horizontally. To one of these a donkey was attached; to the others, large stones that ground the ore to fine mud, for water had been put in, and about 2 oz. of quicksilver. The latter settles in the crevices between the paving stones of the bottom of the pit and collects the particles

9

*of gold. It is finally taken out, tied up in a buckskin bag, and
placed in a crucible. When the mercury is burned off, another
crucible is inserted over the first to re-collect the mercury sub-
limed. Around this mill we found the richest specimens of iron
ore that had been dug out with the gold.*

Leaving Dolores, Abert proceeded south over a steep mountain trail to
the settlement of New Placer, near the present ghost town of Golden, where
strikes of gold, silver, and copper had been made in 1832. Here was the same
cheerless scene of unrelieved hardship. Taking advantage of water from winter snows, some 2,000 people had congregated, living all day underground
and crawling forth in the evening to sell the product of their labor and dine
on a pot of thin *atole* (corn meal mush).

The gold boom in the Ortiz Mountains south of Cerrillos subsided by
the mid-nineteenth century. By and large it had been a hard-scrabble operation pursued by poor Hispanos who endured privation and employed the
rudest of methods to wrest a slim reward from their claims. But a new surge
of excitement, a new bonanza, was just around the corner, this time north
of the Galisteo Basin in the Cerrillos Hills. This venture, however, was to
have an altogether different character. Experienced hardrock miners from
Colorado were in the vanguard and close on their heels came politicians from
Santa Fe and wealthy investors from the East whose business noses told them
quick fortunes were to be made by those shrewd enough to get their stakes
out early. In the end the strike proved less spectacular and enriching than
its initial promise. But withal there was enough glamor, violence, and easy
money to carve out a startling and fascinating history in a short span of
years.

V

Early in the spring of 1879, a prospector fresh from the boom town of Leadville, Colorado, wandered south from Santa Fe and with hammer and pick began testing rock in the foothills of Cerrillos. When he turned up a streak of silver-lead ore, he staked a claim, called it the "Galena Chief," and went to work. As earth was moved and the richness of the strike became apparent, the miner put in a call to friends at Leadville where prospects had already started to decline. Word leaked out and a rush to the Cerrillos district began.

Within weeks a thousand miners were at the scene, tent cities sprang up, saloons were dispensing refreshment across plank counters, and the ring of hammer and drill on stone echoed across the piñon flats and from canyons in the hills. At the beginning, these experienced Leadville men called a meeting to define formally the Cerrillos Mining District, establish the boundaries, and lay out the rules governing the location of claims. All this was done in accordance with the U.S. Mining Laws and its purpose was to insure that development of the area's mineral resources should proceed in an orderly manner. (See Appendix A)

One of the collection of miners' tents south of the main activity became the new community of Cerrillos. March 8, 1879 was officially declared Founder's Day, but it is known that some kind of settlement had existed on the site prior to this date for a school was there as early as 1875. That Cerrillos quickly mushroomed in size and population and became the principal supply point for the area was largely due to the arrival of the main line of the Santa Fe Railroad in 1881.

By 1885 William G. Ritch, former secretary of the Territory, could speak with guarded optimism about the future of Cerrillos:

A mining camp as a general thing is over-rated — it has been so since mining began — and like all excitements, it brings thousands of people from every part of the globe, who expect to become millionaires as soon as they land in the camp. This district, like all others, has had its ups and downs; but the time is fast approaching when the great mystery will be solved. There are good mines here, and those that will pay, and they are being brought to light as fast as means will permit. It is a well known fact that the mineral, as a general rule, lies buried deep, but it has been found in some instances on the surface. Taking into consideration the amount of development that has been done and the amount of capital expended, it will be found that this district has produced more paying mineral to the square inch than most mining districts, other things being equal. During the past two years, coal has been found in very large quantities, and of a first-class quality.

The presence of the railroad meant that demand for coal was especially great. The deposits spoken of by Ritch were uncovered in the foothills of the Ortiz Mountains and a new camp there, known first as Coal Banks and later as Madrid, began to attract miners. At its peak, Madrid claimed a population of 700 miners plus their families. The Colorado Iron and Fuel Company eventually purchased these coal mines and built a railroad spur over the three miles separating Madrid from Cerrillos.

With development of mining in the late '80s and early '90s, Cerrillos flowered into a real town. Enthusiastic boosters saw to the laying out of streets and lots, and on one occasion a festive all-day auction was held to encourage the sale of property. An excursion train brought prospective buyers from Santa Fe and in the excitement one hundred lots were sold in the space of a few hours. In 1892 the Cerrillos Land Company developed a total of 1,000 lots and sold them briskly at $40.00 each.

The town seemed to show such promise that citizens began to wonder if the territorial capital should not be moved to Cerrillos. They were sure a new penitentiary, which was being contemplated, ought to be located in their community because of the accessibility of fine building stone quarries. But in the end the penitentiary went to Santa Fe and the territorial capital remained where it was. The stone was cut and used, but mainly for new businesses in Cerrillos. Quientus Monier, a contracter, did come down from Santa Fe in 1894 and arrange for the quarrying of blocks to be used for coping around the plaza there. The stone was taken from a canyon on the old road to the White Ash mill and mine, one and a quarter miles north of Cerrillos.

Merchants were attracted to the town along with miners. In the 1880s twelve businessmen arrived from Dallas and set up shop. A smithy, bakery, hardware, grocery stores and a barber shop appeared. Barbers Van Allen and Leahy proclaimed themselves "tonsorial artists." The local paper reported, *"Jimmy Leahy is cleaning up and otherwise improving his barber shop. There are no flies in the shop now and there never were any on Jimmy."*

To nourish the residents after a hard day in the mines, Arnold & Stinson's Market unabashedly announced that, *"Our choice fresh meats and game in season act on the digestive organs in a manner most satisfactory, and we are warranted, if cooked as directed, to relieve that tired feeling. There are hundreds of people who testify in glowing terms as to their superfine quality."* For those not inclined to patronize the market there was Scranton's Short Order House, whose menu boasted porterhouse steak at 50 cents and sirloin at 35 cents.

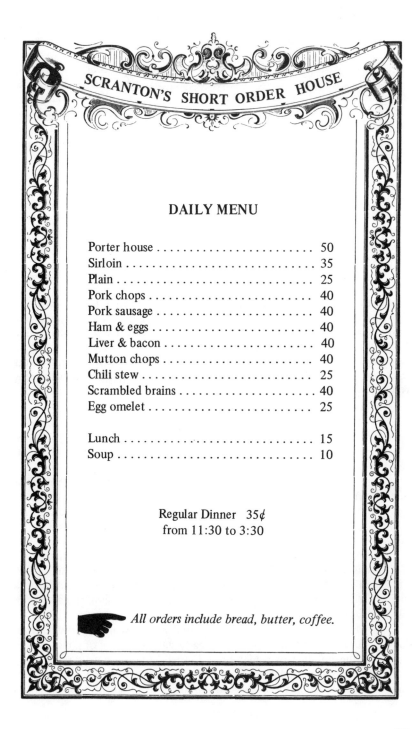

SCRANTON'S SHORT ORDER HOUSE

DAILY MENU

Porter house 50
Sirloin 35
Plain 25
Pork chops 40
Pork sausage 40
Ham & eggs 40
Liver & bacon 40
Mutton chops 40
Chili stew 25
Scrambled brains 40
Egg omelet 25

Lunch 15
Soup 10

Regular Dinner 35¢
from 11:30 to 3:30

All orders include bread, butter, coffee.

Harry Scranton not only fed miners at moderate prices, but he also managed the Cerrillos baseball team, the Little Pittsburghs. Spirited games were played against teams from Albuquerque, Bernalillo and Santa Fe, but the greatest heat was reserved for the neighboring rival, the Madrid Blues. On one occasion, a string of losses prompted Manager Scranton to reveal that he had ordered 3,000 sheets of sticky fly paper to be worn on the catching mitts and the soles of the baseball shoes. He placed a sample of the fly paper on display in Leahy's Barber Shop to inspire home team rooters.

One of the town's leading business establishments was the Cerrillos Supply Company. To this giant emporium came the miners from the surrounding hills to stock up on all the assorted equipment required in their operations: shovels, picks, and similar tools, general hardware, steel, fuses and blasting caps and the various articles needed to make a comfortable camp, such as sheet metal stoves, buckets, kettles, bake ovens, rope and tents. Recognizing the inevitability of accidents in the mines, the Company thoughtfully provided a complete line of undertaking supplies.

Travelers from afar could reach Cerrillos via the railroad, but visitors to outlying mining areas were dependent upon stagecoach service or livery hacks. The firm of Cochran & Williams owned the Cerrillos Livery and Stage Line that operated a daily coach to and from the San Pedro mines at Golden. It also maintained a four horse coach and express that departed Cerrillos for the Cochiti Mining District on Mondays and Thursdays. The principal towns there were Allerton and Bland and people going to these places usually took a stage from Santa Fe to Cerrillos where they transferred to the Cochran & Williams line.

As Cerrillos thrived it acquired several newspapers, among them the *Cerrillos Rustler, Prospector, Comet, Register, Galisteo, Democrat, Beacon* and *Chronicle.* All were small tabloids of a few sheets. Each had a life of several years, then quietly folded without making any notable splash in the world of frontier journalism.

Any roughneck mining town in the territory could claim more than the usual number of saloons, dance halls and pool rooms, and Cerrillos was not remiss in supporting a respectable contingent of such pleasure palaces. At the height of the mining fever, twenty-seven saloons offered refreshment to the men from the hills and the smelters, and it was a rare Saturday night that failed to witness a brawl or a shooting. One of the better patronized grog parlors was Pat Hogan's Saloon which advertised 5 cent beer and "Free Lunch" in its window. Hogan's probably occupied the building that now houses the Melodrama Theater. Other saloons offered a shot of whiskey for three pinches of gold dust.

A sobering effect was provided by fundamentalist preachers who occasionally stumped the town. And at an early date a handful of pious citizens supported the building of a Methodist Church. Catholics were served by a priest who visited periodically from Peña Blanca or Santa Fe. The present San José Church was not built until the 1920s.

Nor was education neglected. In 1892 the Cerrillos School Board erected a two-story building of locally quarried stone. It could boast the first central heating furnace in any school in New Mexico. A well-known educator, Professor Flavio Silva, was engaged to instruct the Spanish-speaking children, while John M. Barnhart became the first principal of the new school. Wayward moppets of the miners long remembered one notorious teacher who disciplined miscreants by hurling books and slates at them.

Before the turn of the century at least four hotels did a lively business in Cerrillos. Perhaps the oldest was the Harkness Hotel, an eighteen-room frame building facing the railroad tracks. It was established by D.D. Harkness who moved his family to Cerrillos from Las Vegas in 1880. In that year railroad track was being laid and Mrs. Harkness was persuaded to board the foreman and six of the men employed in constructing the road bed. She told her husband on his return home from a trip, *"Well, Pa, I've started a hotel. I have seven boarders."*

More luxurious than the Harkness was the Palace Hotel, a rambling edifice of stone and adobe that stood on the western edge of town. The builder of the Palace was an ambitious pioneer named Richard Green who brought his family west from North Carolina by wagon train. The Greens first settled at the San Pedro copper mines near Golden, where the father and the three oldest sons obtained a contract to haul ore to Cerrillos and the railroad. Green soon moved his wife and children to Cerrillos, gave up freighting and began construction of the building that would become the Palace Hotel. The rock section, consisting of twelve rooms, was built first with the stone mason being paid $5.00 a day. Later additions were made of adobe, and the final cost of the completed hostelry is estimated to have been $10,000.

In addition to sheltering the large Green family and regular guests, the Palace Hotel also provided offices and quarters for the town physician. Dr. Friend Palmer,* and for a dentist, Dr. William Bishop. A special guest room was honored by the presence of such notables as Ulysses S. Grant, Thomas A. Edison and Territorial Governor L. Bradford Prince. Edison spent a brief period in Cerrillos conducting experiments in an attempt to extract gold from sand and gravel by static electricity. Another guest, a chemist from the Cash Entry mine, hanged himself upstairs in Room 10 during the 1890s. The manager boasted in his advertising: *"For a good meal, nice rooms, and every convenience travelers will find the Palace Hotel the place to stop. The rates are reasonable and every attention is paid to the wants of guests."* In 1906 Richard Green died and his famous hotel closed soon after.

*The burly and good-natured Dr. Palmer consumed whiskey for his own ailments, reserving patent medicines for his patients. He was especially fond of burro meat.

A major fire swept down Railroad Avenue in 1890 destroying thirteen buildings in the heart of Cerrillos. The firefighters could do little to control the blaze because of the scarcity of water. The town depended on a single well and water from it sold for 25 cents a barrel. Railroad Avenue was rebuilt later and the Santa Fe line installed a waterworks for its own use and that of the community.

The prosperity of Cerrillos was short-lived. The decline of the mines beginning about 1900 led to a rapid exodus of the population. In 1904, when a special election was called to disincorporate the town, only 31 voters cast ballots. (Appendix B) But Cerrillos refused to die. Instead it lingered on, much reduced in size and diminished in spirit, but dreaming still of the days when it was the belle of the New Mexico Territory.

Cerrillos buildings with a look of the Old West.

A Cerrillos street scene today including the famous Tiffany Saloon. (Photo by Marc Simmons)

Hauling water by mule team. Cerrillos in the 1890s.

An early business in Cerrillos. Notice attempt to correct the spelling of
"bakery."

The old stagecoach road over Devil's Throne to Waldo.

A Fourth of July celebration in Madrid, with a little air pollution in the background.

Empty houses of miners in Madrid. (Photo by Buddy Mays)

Rock formations in the "Little Garden of the Gods" east of Cerrillos.

Fires were frequent in Madrid.

Loading coal at Madrid. Famous engine "Uncle Dick" in the foreground.

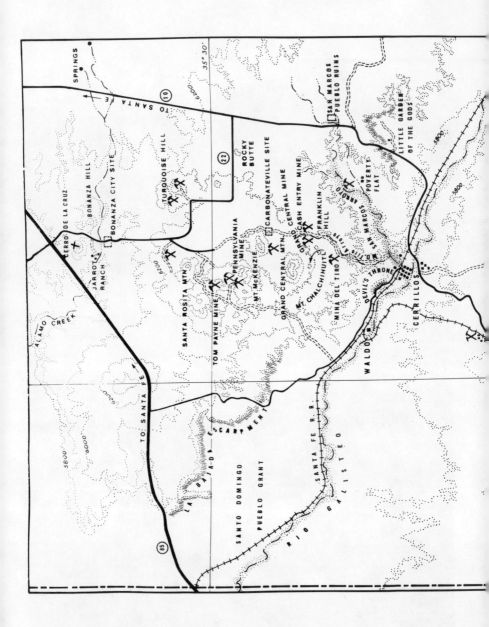

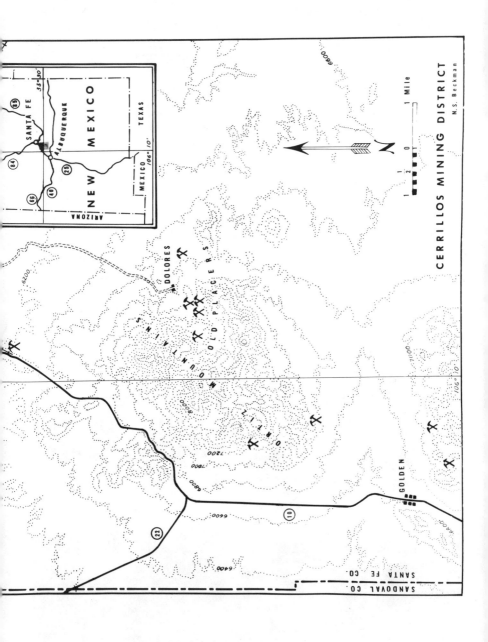

CERRILLOS MINING DISTRICT

N.S. Beckman

The Tom Paine Mine, one of the most productive in the Cerrillos District. (Photo by Bart Durham)

Miner's camp at the Ruelina shaft near Cerrillos in the 1880s. Note men clustered around mine entrance and windlass, upper right.

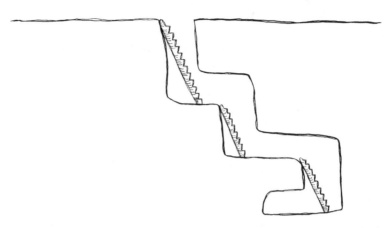

Figure 1. Indian "Chicken Ladders" in a stair-step mine shaft as described by early visitors to the Cerrillos District. *(Frank Turley)*

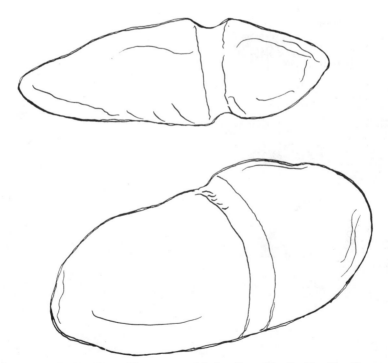

Figure 2. Indian Stone Hammers or Mauls. Found in the Cerrillos Turquoise Mines. *(Frank Turley)*

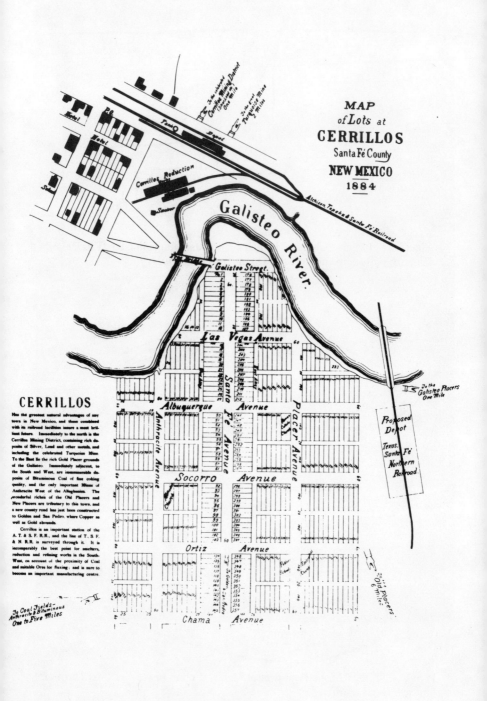

MAP
of Lots at
CERRILLOS
Santa Fé County
NEW MEXICO
1884

Atchison Topeka & Santa Fé Railroad

Galisteo River

Galisteo Street.

Las Vegas Avenue

Albuquerque Avenue

Socorro Avenue

Ortiz Avenue

Chama Avenue

Santa Fé Avenue

Anthracite Avenue

Placer Avenue

Cerrillos Reduction

Smelter

To the Gahsteo Placers
One Mile

Proposed Depot

Texas, Santa Fé Northern Railroad

To Coal Fields
Anthracite & Bituminous
One to Five Miles

Old Placers
Six Miles

CERRILLOS

Has the greatest natural advantages of any town in New Mexico, and these combined with its railroad facilities insure a most brilliant future. Immediately to the north is the Cerrillos Mining District, containing rich deposits of Silver, Lead and other metals, and including the celebrated Turquoise Mine. To the East lie the rich Gold Placer grounds of the Galisteo. Immediately adjacent, to the South and West, are inexhaustible deposits of Bituminous Coal of fine coking quality, and the only important Mines of Anthracite West of the Alleghanies. The wonderful riches of the Old Placers and New Placers are tributary to this town, and a new county road has just been constructed to Golden and San Pedro, where Copper as well as Gold abounds.

Cerrillos is an important station of the A. T. & S. F. R.R., and the line of T. S. F. & N. R.R. is surveyed through it. It is incomparably the best point for smelters, reduction and refining works in the South-West, on account of the proximity of Coal and suitable Ores for fluxing; and is sure to become an important manufacturing centre.

Hurt's old opera house in Cerrillos.

Pupils and teachers pose in front of the old Cerrillos school.

Young ladies in their Sunday best, at the Cerrillos depot.

The Cerrillos smelter, probably about 1902.

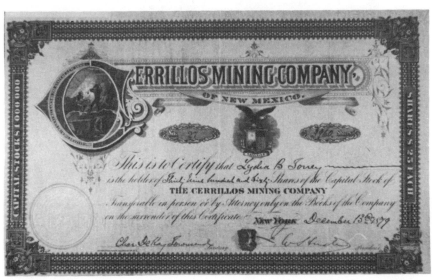

A Cerrillos mining certificate, dated 1879, the first year of the boom.
(L. Bradford Prince Papers, New Mexico State Records Center & Archives)

The Green Family plot in the Cerrillos cemetery. At left, grave of Richard Green, pioneer freighter and builder of the Palace Hotel.

VI

Cerrillos was always the hub of the mining district south of Santa Fe, but lesser satellite communities also played their role in the turbulent history of this colorful area. Dolores, or El Placer, was the oldest camp, but its glory had faded by the middle of the nineteenth century. Nevertheless, a few diehards continued to scratch out a living in its depleted gold fields for another fifty years and a post office was maintained there until 1901.

Further south the New Placers at San Pedro and Golden (known originally as El Real de San Francisco) continued active well into the present century, the population there once numbering 6,000. Gold was the original magnet but, as it played out, the discovery of copper gave a new lease on life to these settlements. In the early days spectacular finds of large nuggets were occasionally made. A huge chunk of yellow metal, weighing eleven pounds nine ounces, was discovered by a Pueblo Indian who traded it off for a little whiskey, a blind pony and a hat.

Exploration showed that with sufficient water for sluicing a fortune in gold could be taken from the gravel of the New Placers. Several enterprising gentlemen surveyed the problem and announced that for a mere $400,000 a ditch could be constructed from the Rio Grande 20 miles away and water brought to the site. But the enormity of this sum prevented the plan from ever advancing beyond talk.

Of the towns below Cerrillos, Madrid proved the most prosperous and enduring. Investment by big companies and the railroad in its coal fields meant steady employment and a substantial payroll that spelled municipal prosperity. For many years, in fact as late as the 1930s, the pride of Madrid was its annual Christmas display, a spectacle attracting sightseers from distant places and giving pleasure to the local mining families. Graying frameworks of wood that once held festive holiday lights still stand as decaying relics on summits of the low hills that box in the town on all sides.

Another break in the year, which lightened the toil and drudge of coal mine labor at Madrid, was the annual Fourth of July celebration. Washtubs of pink lemonade slaked the thirst of townsfolk and visitors from Cerrillos and Santa Fe and a parade led by the miners' band provided diversion. Fireworks were lacking, but mine blacksmiths could always be counted upon to "shoot" their anvils. They did this by setting one anvil on another with a charge of gunpowder between them. A lighted fuse produced a thundering boom, sending the top anvil 20 feet into the air. Spectators kept a respectful distance from these noisy demonstrations.

Yet the gaiety of such holidays was overshadowed by the disasters that seemed to plague Madrid with relentless regularity. Mine explosions were common and created new widows and orphans each year. The fire attending one such tragedy could not be quenched, so the shaft was sealed and a veritable devil's furnace was left to blaze for decades underground.

One winter's afternoon the children of Madrid attending school in Cerrillos looked from their classroom windows in horror to see a huge cloud of black smoke filling the sky. Then they heard the low rumble of the explosion and felt the deep tremor resembling an earthquake. *"It's the mines. It's the mines,"* they screamed. And they raced from the building, scattering and scrambling tearfully over the rocky hills toward home and disaster. More than 30 miners lost their lives that day.

The town of Madrid itself, with its lanes of tinder-dry wooden residences, was constant prey to the ravages of fire. One blaze in the 1920s was touched off in an extraordinary manner. Some water pipes had frozen and in an attempt to thaw them a homeowner put his blowtorch to work. He thoughtlessly left the flame unattended and a spark set the house afire. The superintendent of the mines was summoned and he decided that the flaming building should be dynamited at one corner so that it would topple into a nearby arroyo out of harm's way. The theory may have appeared sound but the result proved otherwise. The explosion sent blazing timbers raining down upon adjacent structures and a third of the town was destroyed in the ensuing conflagration.

The village of Waldo, two miles northwest of Cerrillos, lay at the junction of the spur line from Madrid and the main Santa Fe track. It was named for the chief justice of the Territorial Supreme Court, Judge Henry L. Waldo. A famous engine, the "Uncle Dick" (after Dick Wootten, first to cross Raton Pass), hauled shuttle cars from the Madrid mines and the coal was either treated in the Waldo coke ovens or was shifted directly to the main line for shipment. As little more than a railroad junction and a wide place on the alternate Cerrillos-to-Santa Fe stagecoach road, Waldo possessed few attractions to larger settlement, and by the 1920s it had withered away to become another ghost town of the Cerrillos Hills.

The community of Carbonateville, later called Turquesa, was situated on the main wagon road three miles north of Cerrillos. Some of the Leadville miners settled here in 1879, among them James Morris, to whose family the first child was born in the camp. Also of the group was Mike O'Neill, who staked and worked a large number of claims and later joined with Governor L. Bradford Prince in local mining ventures. Another territorial governor, General Lew Wallace (1878-1881), reputedly vacationed at the hotel in Carbonateville and while there wrote certain chapters of his immortal novel, *Ben Hur*.

William Ritch declared in 1883: *"Carbonateville is now a flourishing village, and when reduction works are put up in this vicinity, the camp will be the scene of great activity."* Part of his enthusiasm for the place may be traced to a discovery of the previous year as reported by the *Santa Fe New Mexican* (June 23, 1882):

> *The owners of the carbonate mine which is located just above Carbonateville in the Cerrillos district were made happy yesterday by the announcement that some fine ore had been struck at a depth of one hundred and seventy feet. The mine always showed fair ore which would pay for the work, and now a body of minerals has been unearthed which will run six hundred dollars to the ton. There seems to be a quantity of it, and the mine has risen very materially in the estimation of the owners and everybody else since the new strike has been made.*

At its height the town counted a population of 600. But any hope for a real future was thwarted by the lack of water. All water had to be laboriously hauled in barrels by wagon from springs several miles away. Carbonateville may have been abandoned by the mid-1880s. In any case, it is known that when the Tiffany Company of New York obtained an interest in the nearby turquoise mines, it established a new post office and a superintendent's office on or near the site of Carbonateville and called the place Turquesa.

Three miles beyond Carbonateville on the road to Santa Fe, Bonanza City was founded in the spring of 1880. Its location was more favorable, in a grassy and well-watered swale not far from the site of the old Pino hacienda.

One of the earliest citizens, a Colonel Mahoney, who had served as consul to Egypt during President Grant's administration, built a luxurious residence and invested heavily in the adjacent mines. Other mining barons were Edward F. Bennett and John Andrews, owners of turquoise claims and members of the North American Mining Company.

Although Bonanza City rose to 2,000 inhabitants, its life proved as ephemeral as that of neighboring towns. When the mines played out, there was nothing left to hold the people. Boarding up their homes and stores, they moved to new camps just opening in the southern part of the Territory. In 1883 the Bonanza City post office closed and the town began to melt back to dust.

VII

A hallmark of any mining town is lawlessness. Men who sink shafts and break rock are a tough, hard-drinking lot and at the fringes of such crews can always be found the saloon-keepers, the gamblers and the shady characters who see a chance for easy profit skimmed off the labor of others. Mines mean money, and money, like honey, draws the drones. Cerrillos and the other towns were no strangers to the violent mold and gents quick with their fists or a six-gun wrote a sanguine chapter in the history of this ebullient mining district.

Black Jack Ketchum was the most famous and perhaps the bloodiest outlaw to operate in the Galisteo Basin and environs. According to some reports, an attempt he made to rob the Santa Fe Railroad was foiled and he suffered a gunshot wound. Carried to Dr. Palmer's office in Cerrillos' Palace Hotel, the would-be train bandit bled copiously on the floor, leaving a stain that could still be seen in 1968 when the building burned. Black Jack survived that escapade only to be hanged for murder at Clayton a few years later.

The saloons and dance halls of Cerrillos witnessed their share of mayhem, much of it caused for a time by rivalry among the rougher element for the favor of a popular madam, Bronco Mary. On one memorable evening a couple of Mary's suitors met in the street to decide who was the better man, letting their six-guns be the judge. *"I'll shoot you down like a dog,"* yelled one, and he opened fire, killing his opponent instantly. After the encounter, he attempted to escape, but within minutes was arrested by the town constable. Apparently officers of the law did not regard this as an acceptable manner for settling disputes.

Another serious episode occurred in a Cerrillos gambling den. Gold, cash and cards lay spread upon the green cloth and a miner, disgruntled by a streak of bad luck, eyed his fellow players suspiciously. Suddenly and in an ominous tone, he called the dealer, told him he was a crook and a tinhorn. *"No man can call me a cheat and live,"* declared the dealer. But his draw was slower than his challenge. As the miner drilled him, he slumped face down on the table. And the bullet kept going, killing an innocent man sitting behind.

Susan Wallace, wife of the Governor, set out with a group of friends in an army ambulance in the early '80s to have a view of the Cerrillos turquoise mines. On an isolated stretch of road, the party unexpectedly met the notorious desperado Texas Jack, the mere sight of whose wolfish person was sufficient to inspire terror. Mrs. Wallace, more fascinated than alarmed, described him as:

*a powerful fellow, of giant frame and dangerous muscle, and
even unarmed a foe to dread in any fight. A shaggy unshorn
mane, reddened with dust and sunburn, fell over the buffalo
neck and shoulders; matted beard, a very jungle, reached almost
to the cartridge belt, and blown aside by the wind, revealed the
outline of revolvers in his breast pocket. He carried a Winchester
rifle as easily as a gentleman carries a cane; a leather belt, buckled
around his waist, was filled with cartridges, and bore a murderous
looking knife in its sheath.*

Fortunately for the lady and her companions, Texas Jack was not bent
on mischief that day. *"The frontiersman,"* she says, *"touched his hat-brim
with his big forefinger, sunburnt to a vermillion red, quietly passed on toward
the Galisteo, and we saw him no more. When fairly out of sight of the
outlaw, we felt brave as lions."* Tense jokes were made, but all knew they
had experienced a close call.

If the sum of deviltry that went on in the Cerrillos mining camps could
be fully totaled, it would no doubt present an appalling figure. As in all
places on our western frontier, the honest citizenry strove to preserve itself,
its property and some measure of justice. One such effort was recorded by
a Santa Fe newspaper in September of 1880:

*At Carbonateville on Monday night, a meeting of the miners was
held for the purpose of organizing a Miners Protective Associa-
tion. Dennis Carflin presided. A committee was appointed to
prevent the carrying of weapons and shooting in the camp, the
residents of the place having been disturbed by drunken men
shooting after dark. No other business was transacted, but
another meeting will be held soon at which the Protective Associ-
ation will be put on a firm basis.*

Even while this plan was in preparation, a crime of passion shocked the
folk of Carbonateville. The central figure in the affair was an unsavory
specimen, sporting a mustache and goatee, by the name of E.M. Kelly, alias
Choctaw Kelly. He had come out of Texas by way of Las Vegas to the
country below Santa Fe. According to reports that preceded him, *"he was
a lawless individual, a former cowboy who, when under the influence of
liquor, was known as a bad and pugnacious man."*

Choctaw Kelly staked some claims, grubbed in the earth and found
nothing. In Cerrillos he opened a dance hall — his real interest was in such
business — but it too failed, and he closed the doors heavily in debt. Next
he got on the payroll of one of the local mining companies and apparently
did well enough to liquidate the claims against him with enough left over to
open another hall and saloon in Carbonateville. A hard fellow called
Thompson was his partner in this new venture.

One afternoon Kelly patronized one of his competitors, the Abbott
Saloon, and there became drunk and unruly. He picked a fight with a popular miner, John Reardon, and the two exchanged harsh words. In anger Kelly

drew a knife and rushed at Reardon, but was pulled back by several by-standers. Thompson then came in, got mixed in the quarrel, and threatened Reardon's life. Stopped from wielding his knife, Choctaw Kelly flew out the door raging and ran to his dance hall where he secured a Winchester rifle.

Several of Reardon's friends warned him to leave, but he would hear nothing of flight. Kelly returned and pointed his rifle at the miner's head. Reardon knocked the weapon aside, but it discharged, delivering a mortal wound in the side. The local magistrate promptly arrested both Kelly and Thompson.

The town was stunned. Reardon had been a hard-working and re-spected citizen, while the murderer and his friend were generally held in low esteem. *"Hang 'em! Hang 'em both,"* went the cry throughout Carbonate-ville. To avert a lynching, the magistrate placed his two prisoners under strong guard and hurried them off to Santa Fe for safety.

Thompson was eventually cleared and released, but his partner was sentenced to hang. A gallows was raised in the arroyo near the military cemetery and Reardon's friends from the Cerrillos district came up to the capital to be certain it was strong enough to do the work. But at the last moment President Chester A. Arthur commuted Kelly's sentence to life imprisonment. The Carbonateville miners talked of storming Santa Fe and carrying out their original plan of lynching. However, when the Governor threatened to call out the militia to protect the prisoner, the rumbling sub-sided, and Choctaw Kelly disappeared behind the brick walls of the territorial prison.

VIII

Turquoise mines in the Cerrillos Hills added a distinctive flavor to the history of this district. The site of the most extensive prehistoric mining operation in America was situated on Mount Chalchihuitl where aboriginal workers carved out a pit from solid rock measuring 200 feet in depth and resulting in the removal of 100,000 tons of waste rock. Several of these pits or open turquoise mines occur in the uplands north of modern Cerrillos, but the one on the eastern slope of Mount Chalchihuitl was in all respects the most imposing. The word *chalchihuitl*, which derives from *xiuitl*, signifying "turquoise" in the Aztec language, was introduced by the Spaniards and their Indian servants from central Mexico. Ancient stone hammers and potsherds found around the diggings indicate they were worked by the native people for perhaps a thousand years.

Cerrillos turquoise was famous far and wide among native Americans. As an article of trade it found its way into the southeastern United States, northward into Canada, and as far south as middle Mexico and the Mayan area. According to legend, the powerful Aztec emperor Montezuma II went about bedecked in necklace and pendants of turquoise from the remote Cerrillos deposits.

To the Tano and other Pueblo Indians who extracted the blue stones, turquoise was highly prized for use as ornaments or as votive offerings to the gods. It was thought to symbolize good fortune and to insure a long and healthful life. At prehistoric Pueblo Bonito in northwestern New Mexico, archaeologists have recovered some 50,000 pieces of turquoise, more than half of it in the form of beads. Experts have concluded that Cerrillos was the chief source of this stone.

It is difficult to judge how much attention the early Spaniards gave to the turquoise mines. Coronado was given blue stones at Pecos Pueblo a few leagues east of the Galisteo Basin and he gathered specimens from other villages, but this was scarcely compensation for the gold he had expected to find. Perhaps part of his collection went to enrich the crown jewels of Spain as popular legend claims. Explorers who came after him often commented on the fine turquoise they observed among the Indians, but it appears to have excited no unusual interest.

In the 1620s Father Zárate Salmerón reported on mineral deposits around San Marcos Pueblo and elsewhere in New Mexico, noting that:

[the] Spaniards that are there are too poor in capital to work the deposits, and are of less spirit: enemies to work of any sort. In the country we have seen silver, copper, lead,. . .and mines of turquoise which the Indians work in their paganism, since to them it is as diamonds and precious stones. At all this the Spaniards who are there laugh; as they have a good crop of tobacco to smoke, they are very content, and wish no more riches.

One story associated with the turquoise mines sounds wholly improbable, but it has been told so often and for so long that it may contain some germ of truth. According to its main outline, the Spaniards enslaved a number of Pueblo Indians to work in the mines of Cerrillos where a cave-in causing many deaths was the spark which touched off the terrible blood bath of 1680. After the expulsion of the Spaniards, the Indians concealed the mines and thereafter kept their location secret.

Of the many versions of this yarn, that given by Susan Wallace is representative:

The tradition is that the chalchihuite *mines, through immemorial ages known to the primitive races, were possessed by the Spaniards in the sixteenth century. Indian slaves then worked them under the lash of the conqueror until 1680, when, by accident, a portion of the rock fell and killed thirty Pueblos. The Spaniards immediately made a requisition on the town of San Marcos for more natives to take their places; when, with a general uprising, they drove the hated oppressor from the country as far south as El Paso. I give the tale for what it is worth.*

Unobtrusively, Pueblo Indians of the upper Rio Grande Valley continued to extract turquoise from the Cerrillos deposits until the 1870s when the area was enveloped by the mining boom. Although silver and traces of gold were chiefly responsible for luring prospectors, interest soon extended to the old turquoise workings. When it appeared that the blue stone might be present in sufficient quantity to make its mining commercially profitable, Santa Fe politicians, notably a succession of territorial governors, entered into schemes to gain control and exploit the most promising claims. Under their leadership, a great deal of money, much of it invested by eastern syndicates, went into elaborate development plans. As in any speculative venture, a few persons made substantial profits, while many suffered losses and disappointment.

One immediate difficulty arose from litigation growing out of claims dating back to a Spanish land grant of 1728. Another appeared when the Tiffany Company of New York, after investing some $100,000 in exploration, discovered that the oldest and most famous turquoise digging on Mount Chalchihuitl had been largely exhausted by the Indians and contained little marketable stone.

But blue color was evident elsewhere on the north side of the Cerrillos district and fortune hunters staked one hundred or more turquoise claims. The richest proved to be clustered about a round hill two and a half miles above Carbonateville and a short distance east of Bonanza City. On Turquoise Hill was also found the ancient Castilian Mine, said to have been worked by the Spaniards. The North American Turquoise Company of New York bought up much of this site in the early 1890s. Tiffany's, which had a principal interest in the Company, allegedly took out $2 million worth of gem material between 1892 and 1899.*

Another nearby mine, the Consul Mahoney, produced a high-grade blue turquoise. It was on a standard miner's claim 300 by 1,500 feet and consisted of a shaft 84 feet deep. A horizontal tunnel led to a fissure in gray porphyry rock where a large vein of turquoise was found. Some of this material was sent to experts in New York and Naples in 1886 who found that it compared favorably with the highly-regarded turquoise of Persia.

The belt north of Cerrillos town containing the turquoise mines was a mere eight miles long and two to five miles wide. While syndicates and affluent politicians had most of it sewn up within a few years, a few lucky prospectors now and then made a "find" on one of the smaller claims. Among them was a Mr. Simmons (no relation to the author) who turned up the largest rough turquoise ever found in the district. Nicknamed "Jumbo," it was a sky blue stone as large as a pigeon's egg.

The color of much of the Cerrillos turquoise was the same deep blue evident in Jumbo. This hue was favored over the greenish turquoise found in Grant County and other sites in New Mexico. The stone's principal use was for costume jewelry, but pieces of inferior grade were also in demand for inlay work on cabinets and table tops.

The total value of turquoise mined in the Territory for the early years of the 1890s is shown in the following table. While the figures include production from mines in the Burro Mountains near Silver City and the Jarilla district not far from Las Cruces, the bulk of each figure represents stones taken out of the Cerrillos Hills.

Year	Value
1891	$150,000
1892	175,000
1893	200,000
1894	250,000
1895	350,000
1896	475,000

*Patented mining claims on Turquoise Hill included the Blue Bell, Morning Star, Blue Gem, Muniz, Sky Blue, Castilian and Elisa lode claims.

Apparently these sums fall far short of actual production, and the only thing they show with fair certainty is that gem mining steadily expanded during the decade. One reason true values could not be ascertained was that mine owners habitually underestimated the worth of their property for tax purposes. For example, in 1892 holders of one of the Cerrillos deposits placed a valuation upon it of $250. The Santa Fe County Commissioners, knowing that the mine had been in constant operation, considered the figure absurdly low. Their ensuing investigation resulted in raising the valuation to $25,000, upon which the owners cheerfully paid the levy. The same mine in 1893 sold for $250,000, and according to rumor brought the new proprietors a million and a half dollars over the next several years. A single stone reputedly sold for $6,000.

All activity surrounding extraction of turquoise was shrouded in the greatest secrecy. The companies never divulged the exact location of their diggings nor the methods they used. No one was allowed to inspect the mines, photographs were forbidden, and employees were prohibited from speaking about their work to outsiders. Governor William T. Thornton (1893-1897) came down from Santa Fe to examine a turquoise property in which he hoped to invest, and even he was denied entrance. Such secrecy helped to hoodwink the tax collector, and allowed several brazen operators to declare that their claims were actually operating at a loss. Much of the blue stone left New Mexico unreported, but one gunnysack was intercepted containing $100,000 worth of turquoise. Part of the control measures of the mine owners could be justified, however. The open pits and shafts were vulnerable to thieves, and while the district was in operation, stealing remained a continuous problem.

Turquoise returned a large profit for the labor and investment involved because of the high value of a small number of gems and because simple and inexpensive methods were adequate for handling the ore. No costly machinery was required nor any complicated treatment for the material removed from the mine. When promising rock was found on the surface, a shaft was sunk until turquoise showed up in paying quantities. Drifting then began; that is, tunnels were run to follow the vein or search for pockets. The rock was blasted and then broken into portable pieces with a sledge hammer. Ore was put into a bucket and hoisted to the top by means of a windlass. Next it was sorted, packed in boxes, and shipped for cutting to jewelry firms in New York that had a contract with the mine owner. Very little turquoise was commercially cut in the Territory.

Wages paid to the Cerrillos turquoise miners were far from magnanimous. The average Mexican worker received $1.50 a day, Anglos got $2.50, an early example of wage discrimination. The largest mines had need of no more than seven to ten men, and in good rock this force could take out up to $10,000 worth of gemstone daily. The miners found the best turquoise in nodules surrounded by lime incrustations. It was most stable and less liable to lose its color upon exposure to dry air or to shatter when being cut.

Some early visitors to the Cerrillos fields observed that Pueblo Indians, particularly those from Santo Domingo, were continuing to work several of the ancient deposits. Most of the prehistoric sites had been open pits, but, perhaps following the lead of the Spaniards, the Indians had taken to working shafts in a stair-step fashion. These were the same kinds of excavation reported by Josiah Gregg among Mexican miners at Dolores in the 1840s. Instead of a straight vertical shaft, platforms or landings were cut from the solid rock at intervals of 12 to 14 feet and were connected by notched poles, called chicken ladders, of the kind used by the Indians in the Pueblos. The ore was broken up with stone hammers and loaded into rawhide bags, which were then carried up the series of ladders on the backs of native miners.

The Indians' right to mine the turquoise was apparently recognized for a time. The Pueblo of Santo Domingo, whose eastern reservation boundary approached the Cerrillos Hills, claimed ownership through a number of its residents who were descended from the early occupants of San Marcos and Galisteo Pueblos. These villages and all others in the Galisteo Basin had been abandoned during Spanish times and their people scattered. Historical records confirm that at least a few took up residence at Santo Domingo on the Rio Grande. Be that as it may, an incident in 1888 led to suspension of all Indian rights over the ancient turquoise diggings.*

The central figure in this small drama was a feisty blue-eyed Irishman named J.P. McNulty. For several years he served as superintendent of the Tiffany turquoise mines, living on the site with his wife and children in a primitive two-room cabin. His most pressing problem concerned the bands of Pueblos who appeared regularly and demanded access to the mines. In an effort to mollify them, he handed out quantities of second grade blue stone, but the Indians wanted to enter and help themselves. This McNulty steadfastly refused.

One morning he set out for Cerrillos to buy ammunition. Jogging along on his paint horse, he was suddenly ambushed by Indians, and a bullet grazed his face. Putting spurs to his mount, he turned around and raced toward home, breathing a prayer that his wife and children were safe. From the crest of a hill, he saw a cloud of smoke in the distance and cried to himself, *"Oh, God, I'm too late. Why did I leave them?"* But drawing near to the cabin, he observed that all was serene. A short distance beyond, near the old Castilian mine, a crowd of Pueblos had built a large fire and were making threatening gestures.

Barricading himself and his family in the building, McNulty took up a rifle and gave his wife a shotgun. Late in the night the intruders attacked, discharging their bows and arrows and guns, but the missiles thudded harmlessly against the cabin walls. The superintendent and his wife fired back into the darkness, aiming more to scare the Indians off than to cause harm.

*In addition to Santo Domingo, the following modern Pueblos are reported to have once mined turquoise in the Cerrillos district: Santa Ana, Cochiti, San Ildefonso and San Felipe.

At dawn they looked out to see that the field was clear. McNulty walked into his front yard and breathed a sigh of relief, although he felt certain the assailants would return. As he started in to breakfast, he noticed his dogs were raising a commotion. Investigating, he found they had cornered a large rattlesnake, coiled and buzzing ominously. He reached for a rock to kill it, but the snake was closer and longer than he had thought. It struck him on the hand.

Telling of the incident later, McNulty declared, *"The dogs jumped at the rattlesnake and threw him in the air just at the moment my little girl came out the door. It landed on her, then fell at my feet where I soon killed it. I called to my wife for help, then I split the snake bite crosswise, and she sucked the poison out, or as much as she could."*

Within minutes the superintendent's hand began to swell and ache, and he realized he needed medical attention. Burdened by the thought that the Indians still lurked near the mine, he climbed aboard his horse once again and rode for Cerrillos. There he found Dr. Palmer at his office in the Palace Hotel and had the wound dressed. Before returning home, he called on the sheriff and persuaded him to send several deputies along to protect both his family and the property at the mines.

Back at his cabin, McNulty discovered the Indians skulking about once again. Another assault was beaten off that night with the aid of the deputies' guns, and as before, quiet returned with the sunrise. But this time the Pueblos had taken what they came for. They had entered the mine and carried away much valuable turquoise.

With the conflict ended, at least for the time being, Superintendent McNulty hastened to Santa Fe to ask territorial officials for protection. But much to his amazement he learned that no law existed to prevent the Indians from working the old turquoise mines, since this had been their custom for centuries. However, at the next session of the legislature in 1890, a special act was passed making it a crime for any Pueblo to enter the turquoise claims without permission of the current owners. Unjust, perhaps, to the Indians, but the matter was settled.

Reflecting on the episode decades later, white-haired McNulty philosophized: *"The Indians always thought they had a prior right to those old turquoise mines. And to be truthful I had a hankerin' notion they did, too."*

IX

Silver, not turquoise, sparked the mining fever that swept over the Cerrillos district beginning in 1879. Discovery of this precious metal had already caused rushes to boom camps throughout the American West and had led some poor miners with strokes of luck to become millionaires overnight. One enthusiastic newspaper editor at this time referred to Cerrillos as the *"future Silver Queen of the West."* Such effusive comments helped swell the tide of prospectors who flooded into the hills south of Santa Fe.

This mining district embraced approximately 25 square miles of mineralized country above Cerrillos. While silver was the original magnet attracting prospectors, lead and zinc ores ultimately proved more abundant. Some copper and gold also were mined in small quantities.

From the beginning, stock promoters trumpeted the riches of the Cerrillos discoveries, and many of them, carried away perhaps by their own optimistic predictions, invested heavily in mining development. Territorial Governor L. Bradford Prince (1889-1893), among other prominent persons, sank a great deal of capital into speculative ventures, many of which in the end proved wholly unrewarding.

Although a thousand or more claims were staked in the vicinity of the Cerrillos Hills, extensive shafts were dug on only 50 to 60 of these. William Ritch refers to 55 major mines in the 1880s (Appendix C), and a few more were developed in the following decade. Actually, a handful of top producers, perhaps a half dozen, gave up the bulk of the mineral wealth that came from the district in the short stretch of its active years.

The survey of the mines provided by Ritch mentions 15 sites first worked by the Spaniards. This sounds as if a thriving industry had existed during the colonial period, but strangely, in the Spanish archives still preserved in Santa Fe, no mention of any such activity can be found. There is reference to the working of a lead mine near San Marcos Pueblo during the seventeenth century, but regarding any great quest for silver, the official records are silent. Old shafts with graying timbers, waste dumps with mature pinon trees growing on them, and aged pieces of Spanish mining equipment all discovered by the first Anglo miners confirm that the early colonists did labor here. So we must assume their activity was carried on in secret, no doubt to avoid paying the "royal fifth," the tax collected by the King amounting to one-fifth of all precious metal mined in the New World.

Judged to be the oldest of the original Spanish sites was the Mina del Tiro (Mine of the Shaft), located about a mile and a half south of the Mount Chalchihuitl turquoise diggings. Fayette Jones, who examined its interior in the early years of the present century, described what he found:

The old working consists of an incline shaft of 150 feet and connects with a somewhat vertical shaft of about 100 feet in depth. Extensive drifts of 300 feet connect with various chambers or stopes; these chambers were formed by stoping or mining out the richer ore bodies. The full extent of this old working has never been definitely determined; since the lower depths are covered with water which would have to be pumped out to fully explore the mine.

Another site of colonial origin was the Bottom Dollar mine located in Hungry Gulch. It eventually proved to be one of the most profitable of the Cerrillos group with a layer of silver ore five feet thick. A Santa Fe journal advised its readers on April 21, 1883, of a curious find there.

Messrs. Blonger and Whalen, who have a contract of sinking a shaft in the Bottom Dollar mine, near Cerrillos, made an interesting discovery on Monday last. While working at a depth of 110 feet they dropped into an old tunnel made by the Spaniards no less than 200 years ago and out of the debris they took a number of stone hammers, chisels, and picks and found every evidence that this mine belongs to the same class of silver producing mines as does the Mina del Tiro property, which is the most perfect Spanish mine yet discovered in this part of the country. The owners, who are in Santa Fe, are very much gratified at this evidence of the former value of the Bottom Dollar property.

Three of the largest and most consistent producers in the Cerrillos Hills were the Cash Entry, the Grand Central, and the Tom Paine mines. The first, for example, yielded 500 tons of high grade silver ore in 1886, and 4,500 tons of lead-zinc ore between 1890 and 1903. The Grand Central, like the old Mina del Tiro, had a serious problem with flooding, and parts of it had to be abandoned.

By the turn of the century, the voices prophesying a brilliant and bountiful future for the Cerrillos mining district had been stilled. The most accessible silver veins were exhausted and the rowdy element in the camps had long since departed. A few steady hands continued to prospect for poorer grade ores and to patent claims and several companies exploited the industrial metals, but the old glamour was gone.

The following figures represent the total mineral production for the Cerrillos district between 1904 and 1930:

Copper	*160,620 pounds*
Lead	*842,340 pounds*
Zinc	*1,155,527 pounds*

Since 1930 several firms have conducted commercial operations from time to time in the old mines. Santa Fe Lead Zinc Mines, Inc., for instance, reopened the Black Hornet and Bottom Dollar shafts in the early 1950s, but it shipped only three carloads a month, hardly enough to credit the district with a rebirth. Again in 1960, Kennecott Copper Corporation did some preliminary exploration in the area, but what its drillers discovered, if anything, was never disclosed.

Yet mineral remains. And with the energy crisis and the expanding need for raw materials, mining companies are showing new interest in the bleak hills surrounding Cerrillos. Already the turquoise deposits have been reactivated to meet rising demand, and as in times past, armed guards patrol the mines to exclude visitors. But a new boom — if it comes — will be regulated and orderly. Cerrillos has seen the last of the roisterous, freewheeling life of a wide-open mining camp.

X

Bonanza City, Carbonateville, and Waldo are gone, leaving scarcely a trace. Golden at the New Placers and Madrid are catalogued now as ghost towns, although a handful of people continue to reside at each place. And only Cerrillos, among the communities that once numbered their inhabitants by the thousands, can count a population in the hundreds.

Cerrillos today stands as a sleepy relic of the past. The Palace Hotel has vanished, a victim of arsonists in 1968, but several sprawling old homes dating from the crescendo of the mining boom still grace the edges of town. False-fronted stores, their faces lifted in recent years by film companies from Hollywood, lend an air of the Old West to the two main streets. Some deserted, ruined houses of adobe or *jacal* construction can yet be found, but most of these have been surrendered to an invading army of hippies.

A legion of visitors comes each year to dine or take drinks at the historic bar of the famous Tiffany Saloon, to tour the Old Boarding House with its antique furniture, to prowl among the ore samples and rusted mining tools in the What-Not-Shop, or to chat with the friendly proprietors of the Simoni Store, who are descended from one of the town's original merchants.

Cerrillos slumbers, but a visit there invariably awakens interest in its history and causes one to reflect on those days when the mines flourished and the six-gun helped settle the affairs of men.

APPENDIX

A

CERRILLOS MINING DISTRICT*

Proceedings of a Miners' meeting, held at the mining camp of Dimick and Hart, situated in the South-east corner of Section 32 of Township 15 N. Range S E. in Santa Fe County, Territory of New Mexico, March 27, 1879, for the purpose of defining the limits of a Mining District, also to establish rules and regulations for the governing, the location of mining claims and the working of the same, within said district.

On motion Frank Dimick was appointed Chairman and Robert Hart, Secretary, of the meeting, and the following rules were adopted.

Resolved: That this district, organized under the authority of the laws of Congress and of the Territory of New Mexico, shall be called the mining district of the Cerrillos, and said District shall embrace townships 14 and 15 north of the base line, range 7,8,9 of the N.M. principal meridian.

RULES AND REGULATIONS.

1st. *All claims located prior to this date, having been located under the U.S. mining laws, cannot be reduced in extent, but all lodes hereafter located will be limited to 150 feet on each side of the vein, and 1500 feet along the course thereof.*

2nd. *Each person, who is the owner of an interest in a mining claim shall be entitled to vote in the election of a Recorder chosen at this meeting, to serve until his successor is elected and qualified for which a meeting will be held, annually on the first Monday in September.*

3rd. *The Recorder shall faithfully record all claim notices and deeds of transfer in books kept for that purpose, and shall be entitled to charge and receive the amount of two dollars for each entry, for which he will return a receipt to the party making the application.*

4th. *It shall be the duty of the Recorder to furnish, on the application of any party interested, a certified copy of the records at the same rate.*

5th. *On the application of five persons interested in these mines, it shall be the duty of the Recorder to call a meeting by posting in four conspicuous places within the District, Notices specifying the object of the meeting, at least 15 days prior to the time stated in said Notices.*

*From a typescript in the L. Bradford Prince Collection, New Mexico State Records Center and Archives, Santa Fe.

6th. *In all location of claims, a notice shall be posted thereon with name or names of the locators and the date thereof, at or near the discovery shaft; the same to specify the number of feet claimed in each direction from the notice along the lode; the corners of the claims to be marked by stakes or monuments.*

7th. *In claims hereafter located, a shaft no less than ten feet deep shall be sunk on the vein or lode, within 90 days from the date of location.*

8th. *All notices of the taking of claims shall be recorded in this District, within 90 days from the date thereof. All claims located under the U.S. mining laws will be subjected to the above conditions from this date.*

9th. *In estimating the value of improvements, recognized under the U.S. mining laws, viz: One hundred dollars per annum on each mining claim, labor shall be estimated at four dollars per day.*

On motion Frank Dimick was unanimously elected Recorder.

These rules and regulations will remain in force until altered or amended by the decision of a regular miners' meeting.

On motion the meeting adjourned.

Frank Dimick, Chairman

Robert Hart, Secretary

FORMAL CERTIFICATION OF THE DISINCORPORATION OF CERRILLOS, 1904*

Santa Fe, Feb. 20th, 1904

To the Hon. J.W. Reynolds
  Sect. of the Territory of N.M., City

Sir:

 I have the honor to certify to you that an election held in the town of Cerrillos, New Mex., on the 10th day of February, A.D. 1904 for to disincorporate the town, the following is the result of the votes cast as canvassed by the Hon. Board of County Commissioners on the 15th day of February, A.D. 1904, to wit: Twenty-three (23) ballots against the incorporation. Eight ballots (8) for the incorporation.

      In Witness Whereof, I have hereunto set my hand and affixed the seal of the Board of County Commissioners of Santa Fe County, New Mexico, this 20th day of February, A.D. 1904.

       Celso Lopez [signed]
      Probate Clerk and Ex-Officio Clerk of the Board.

*From a copy in the office of the Secretary of State.

STATISTICS OF MINES IN THE CERRILLOS DISTRICT.

NAME.	Depth of Development—ft.	Silver Assay—Ounces.	Gold Assay—Ounces.	Mill Run—Ounces.	Width of Vein. Feet.	Inch's.	REMARKS.
Atzec	70	111				19	Southern extension of the Marshall Bonanza.
Bourbon	110	40			3		
Bonanza No. 3	340	67		30		20	Has fine machinery.
Bottom Dollar	110	40			2		Old Spanish mine.
Big Bonanza	40	25	1½			12	
Blind Tom	60	34				12	
Boss	60	43			2		Good prospect.
Capital	330	72				20	
Cash Entry	140			100			
Chicago	75	76	$30 00		3	6	Good prospect.
Carbonate	170	1,072				22	
Chester	60	2,815			2		Horn silver.
Cock-of-the-Walk	110	100			4	6	Old Spanish mine.
Darling	43			27		18	Old Spanish mine.
Ethel	170			22	2	6	
Franklyn	65			37	4		Old Spanish mine.
Galena Chief	45	97				20	Old Spanish mine—Splendid prospect.
Gen. Moore	105			83	3		Old Spanish mine—Splendid prospect.
Good Hope	130	377			3	6	
Granite State	63			250	2	9	
Great Western	300			90	1	8	
Grand Review	140	103			2	1	
Hawkeye	110	83		4	4	1	Mina-del-Tero, new extension.
Hub	45	65			2	6	Good.
Inter-Ocean	60	16			2	6	Old Spanish mine—Good.
Iola	50	21				5	Old Spanish mine.
Lucky	80			20			Fair prospect.
Globe-Democrat	80						Good prospect.
Little Joe	45	50	1		3		Prospect.
Little Peter	90	70			2		Low grade, 45 per cent. galena.
Lone Star	6	200			1	10	Extension of Mina del Tero.
Little Emma	100	23			3	2	
Monitor	180			20	4		Old Spanish mine.
Nestor	135		1½		40		Low grade.
Open Sesame	40	72			2		
Pelican	50	36			2	6	Old Spanish mine.
Piñon	103	22			1	8	
Platta Verdi	45	17	½		2	6	Old Spanish mine—Good prospect.
Pole Pick	73	161			2	8	Splendid prospects.
Red Jacket	82	119			3	5	Old Spanish mine—Good prospect.
Grover Cleveland	55	67			3		Old Spanish mine—Ext. Mina del Tero.
Ruealena	150			80	2	9	Old Spanish mine.
Santa Fe	60	60			2	6	
Santa Fe Ring	50	34	1½		1	4	Fair prospect—Some lead.
San Diego	237	16			5		
Sleeping Beauty	112	45			2	6	
St. George	45		3		2		
Sunrise	50	68			3		Good low grade.
Theresa	110	67			1	3	Old Spanish mine—Good.
Virgie Lee	45	34			3		The vein of this mine crops out above the surface from 10 to 12 feet high.
Royal Arch	30		2½		30		
Nick-o-Tine	300	95			1	8	
Marshall Bonanza	130			80	6		It is the same vein as the Nestor.
Kittanning	30			40			Extension of Sleeping Beauty.
B. B. Pears	176	30					45 per cent. lead.
So. Ext. B. B. Pears	80						45 per cent. lead.

D

THE ORTIZ MINE ROBBERY

as told by
NANCY GREEN McCLEARY

Large quantities of gold were taken out of the Ortiz Mine, and regular shipments of gold amalgam were sent to the Denver mint via Cerrillos. George Bailey, the foreman, and Roy Green, an employee of the Ortiz Company, were responsible for the safety of these shipments. On one occasion, Roy was driving the wagon from the mine to the railroad in Cerrillos when he was held up by a masked bandit, who, with the aid of a very persuasive 38 Colt, forced him to throw down the bag of gold.

This particular shipment was a "clean up" of the mill and amounted to approximately $50,000. Roy, fortunately, was sent on his way unharmed, but minus his precious cargo. The bandit then dug a hole and buried his loot for safekeeping, against his return when the news and excitement of the robbery had abated.

The entire affair, however, was witnessed by a sixteen-year-old boy of Cerrillos, Maurice Utt. He had been sitting quietly on the side of the hill watching when the crime took place. After the bandit buried the gold, Maurice calmly dug it up and returned the entire amount to George Bailey at the mine. Company officials paid Maurice the sum of $50 as a reward. The bandit was never apprehended.

SELECTED BIBLIOGRAPHY

Abert, Lt. J.W., *New Mexico Report, 1846-'47* (1962).
_____, *Western America in 1846-1847* (1966).
Andrews, Myrtle, "Flurries of Fortune," *New Mexico Magazine*, (Dec. 1937), pp. 16-17; 40-41. Early life in Cerrillos by the "mail order bride" of a mine owner.
_____, "Smoke Signals," *New Mexico Magazine* (Oct. 1936), pp. 26; 44-45. The story of J.P. McNulty.
Bancroft, Hubert Howe, *History of Arizona and New Mexico* (1889).
Cerrillos Land Grant Papers, Collections of the New Mexico State Records Center and Archives. Santa Fe.
The Cerrillos Rustler, June 29, 1894. In Museum of New Mexico, History Library.
Disbrow, Alan E. and Walter C. Stoll, *Geology of the Cerrillos Area, Santa Fe County, New Mexico* (1957).
Gregg, Josiah, *Commerce of the Prairies* (1954).
Higgins, Phillip, "New Mining Activity Boosts Historic Cerrillos District," *New Mexico Miner and Prospector* (Feb. 1952), pp. 3; 20.
Huber, Joe, *The Story of Madrid, New Mexico* (n.d.).
Johnson, D.W., *The Geology of the Cerrillos Hills, New Mexico* (1903).
Jones, Fayette, *New Mexico Mines and Minerals* (1905). Reprinted 1968 as *Old Mines and Ghost Camps of New Mexico*.
Knaus, Charles L., "Mining Districts of New Mexico," *New Mexico Miner and Prospector*, serially 1951-1952.
McCleary, Nancy Green, "Notes," *New Mexico Historical Review*, vol. 24 (1949), pp. 62-65. History of the Green family and the Palace Hotel.
Nelson, Nels C., *Pueblo Ruins of the Galisteo Basin, New Mexico* (1914).
Pearce, T.M., ed., *New Mexico Place Names* (1965).
Prince, L. Bradford, Collection of documents relating to the Cerrillos mining district, New Mexico State Records Center and Archives, Santa Fe.
Ritch, William G., *Aztlán, Resources and Attractions of New Mexico* (1885). Much on territorial mining.
Snow, David H., "Prehistoric Southwestern Turquoise Industry," *El Palacio*, vol. 79 (1973), pp. 33-51.
Stanley, F., *The Carbonateville (New Mexico) Story* (1966). Contains an account of the Reardon-Kelly affair.
_____, *The Cerrillos (New Mexico) Story* (1965).
"Turquoise Mines," in *The Mining Record* (Trinidad, Colo.), Oct. 28, 1899.
Wallace, Susan E., *The Land of the Pueblos* (1888). Chapters on the Cerrillos turquoise mines.
Zárate Salmerón, Gerónimo de, *Relaciones* (1966).

INDEX OF NAMES